Holiday ★ Histories

# Thanksgiving Day

### Mir Tamim Ansary

Heinemann Library
Chicago, Illinois

© 2002 Reed Educational & Professional Publishing
Published by Heinemann Library,
an imprint of Reed Educational & Professional Publishing,
Chicago, Illinois

Customer Service 888-454-2279
Visit our website at www.heinemannlibrary.com

Designed by Depke Design
Printed and bound at Lake Book Manufacturing

06 05 04 03 02
10 9 8 7 6 5 4 3 2 1

**Library of Congress Cataloging-in-Publication Data**
Ansary, Mir Tamim.
   Thanksgiving Day / Mir Tamim Ansary.
      p. cm. -- (Holiday histories)
Includes bibliographical references and index.
   ISBN 1-58810-224-6
   1. Thanksgiving Day--Juvenile literature. [1. Thanksgiving Day. 2. Holidays.]  I. Title.
   GT4975 .A57 2001
   394.2649--dc21
                              2001000098

**Acknowledgments**
The author and publishers are grateful to the following for permission to reproduce copyright material:
Cover photograph: Corbis
pp. 4, 13, 19, 27 Corbis; p. 5 Tony Freeman/Photo Edit; pp. 6–7 SuperStock; pp. 7B, 9, 16, 17, 18, 20–21, 22, 23, 25B, 26 Granger; pp. 10, 11, 12, 14, 15 North Wind Pictures; pp. 24–25 Gettysburg National Military Park Service; p. 28L A. Ramey/Photo Edit; p. 28R David Young-Wolff/Photo Edit; p. 29 Photo Edit.

Every effort has been made to contact copyright holders of any material reproduced in this book. Any omissions will be rectified in subsequent printings if notice is given to the publisher.

Some words are shown in bold, **like this.** You can find out what they mean by looking in the glossary.

# Contents

# Today Is Thanksgiving Day

Winter is coming. In some places, leaves are falling and skies are gray. Yet a happy feeling fills the air. Why? Because today is Thanksgiving Day.

Families have gathered indoors. People are getting ready for their big dinner. Almost every house is filled with the smell of roasting turkey.

# Thanksgiving in the Past

Turkey is always popular at Thanksgiving. In fact, 50 years ago, turkey was served *only* at Thanksgiving. But what does turkey have to do with "giving thanks?"

The answer goes back to a famous party
held almost 400 years ago. The hosts were
**newcomers** to this land. The guests
were Native Americans.

# The First Americans

Native Americans came from Asia, thousands of years ago. By 1600, they lived all across what is now North America. But few people from Europe lived here at that time.

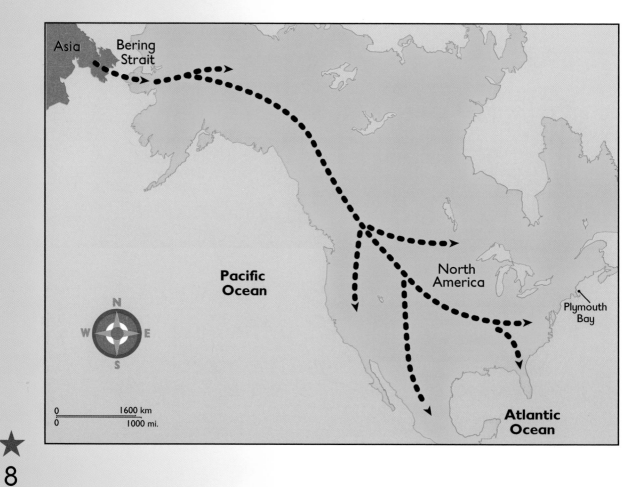

One big Native American tribe was called the Wampanoag. They had about 30 villages along the Atlantic **Coast.** Some lived near a place now known as Plymouth Bay, in Massachusetts.

# The Pilgrims Arrive

One day, a ship sailed into Plymouth Bay. It was called the *Mayflower*. It carried 102 people from England. They wanted to **settle** in North America.

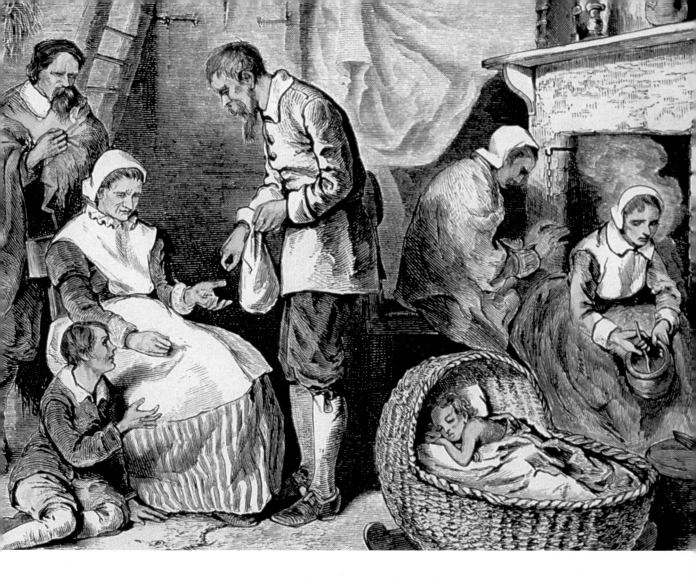

Many of them were pilgrims. A pilgrim
is someone who travels for religious
reasons. The Pilgrims arrived in
North America in November, 1620.

# The Puritan Religion

In England, these pilgrims had been known
as Puritans. They had special ideas about
religion. They believed in **simple** living,
bible study, and prayer.

*Anglican Church in Canterbury, England*

But English law said that everyone must belong to the Anglican Church. This rich church was headed by the king. The Puritans would not join the king's church.

★

# A Search for Freedom

Some Puritans were put in jail for not listening to the king. Others decided to leave the country. But they could not find good homes anywhere in Europe.

*A Puritan who did not listen to the king was sometimes punished by having their hands and head locked in a wooden frame.*

At last, one group decided to try "the New
World"—North America. These were the
people who sailed into Plymouth Bay in
1620. They arrived two months after
leaving Europe.

★

# Hard Times

The Pilgrims did not know how to get food or **shelter** in the new land. By spring, almost half of them had died. Then, some Native Americans came to visit them.

One of these visitors was Massasoit, **chief** of the Wampanoag. Another was Squanto, known then by his Indian name Tisquantum. He lived in Massasoit's village. Tisquantum moved in with the Pilgrims.

# A Good Harvest

Tisquantum taught the Pilgrims how to farm and fish in North America. He taught them how to hunt deer and wild turkeys. By fall, the Pilgrims had plenty of food.

English farmers had a **custom.** After a good **harvest,** they would have a party. The Pilgrims decided to have such a party. They invited the Wampanoag to join them.

# The First Thanksgiving

Celebrating a **harvest** was a Wampanoag **custom,** too. Their holiday was called the Green Corn **Festival. Chief** Massasoit came to the Pilgrim's party with 90 of his people!

One of the main foods at this **feast** was wild turkey. The party lasted for three days. But after it was over, it was mostly forgotten.

# The Thanksgiving Idea

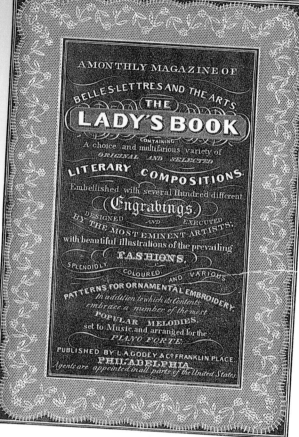

*Sarah Hale wrote for women's magazines like this one.*

In 1840, a writer named Sarah Hale heard about the Pilgrim's **feast.** She wrote about it for magazines. She said the United States should have a Thanksgiving holiday every year.

Hale wrote and spoke about this idea for almost twenty years. At last, President Abraham Lincoln heard what she had to say. Lincoln liked her idea.

*Sarah Hale*

# A Holiday Is Born

At this time, our country was divided by the **Civil War.** Lincoln thought a Thanksgiving holiday might help bring people together.

*President Abraham Lincoln*

In 1863, Lincoln **declared** a **national** Thanksgiving holiday. He set it for the last Thursday in November. He also made it a yearly holiday.

★

# New Americans

After the **Civil War,** new people came to the United States. Like the Pilgrims, many were seeking freedom. These new Americans gladly celebrated Thanksgiving.

These **newcomers** were used to such
a **custom.** Most had **harvest** holidays
where they came from. They helped
make Thanksgiving one of our most
popular holidays.

★

# An American Holiday

Today, Americans come from many different places. Few of us are farmers anymore. Yet most of us celebrate Thanksgiving—and in the same way.

We get together with the people we love.
We give thanks for the good things we
have. Then we sit down together for a
great meal.

# Important Dates

## Thanksgiving Day

| | |
|---|---|
| 1492 | Christopher Columbus first explores the Americas |
| 1607 | First English people **settle** in North America |
| 1620 | Pilgrims arrive at Plymouth Bay, in Massachusetts |
| 1621 | The first Thanksgiving takes place |
| 1789 | George Washington **declares** November 26 a day of **national** thanksgiving |
| 1830 | New York state has an official Thanksgiving Day |
| 1840 | Sarah Hale starts writing about the first Thanksgiving |
| 1863 | Abraham Lincoln declares Thanksgiving a holiday |
| 1865-1900 | More than fourteen million people come to the United States from other countries |
| 1941 | Fourth Tuesday in November named Thanksgiving Day and a national holiday by Congress |

# Glossary

**chief** leader

**Civil War** American war (1861–1865) between the
   Northern states and Southern states

**coast** land near an ocean or sea

**custom** things people always do on special days or
   for certain events

**declare** to announce something

**feast** party at which much is eaten

**festival** time of celebration

**harvest** what a farm grows in a season

**national** having to do with the whole nation

**newcomers** people who have just arrived in a new place

**settle** to make a home in a new place

**shelter** something that covers or protects

**simple** not fancy; plain

# More Books to Read

Bruchac, Joseph. *Squanto's Journey.* New York: Harcourt, 2000.

Kuperstein, Joel. *Celebrating Thanksgiving.* Mankato, Minn.:
   Creative Teaching Press, 1999.

Roop, Connie. *Let's Celebrate Thanksgiving.* Brookfield, Conn.:
   Millbrook Press, Inc., 1999.

# Index

Americans 26–27, 28

Anglican Church 13

Civil War 24, 26

England 10, 12, 13

Europe 8, 14, 15

family 5, 29

Green Corn Festival 20

Hale, Sarah 22–23, 30

harvest 18–19, 20, 27

king 13, 14

Lincoln, Abraham 23, 24, 25, 30

Massasoit 17, 20

*Mayflower* 10

Native Americans 7, 8–9, 16

North America 8, 10, 11,15,18, 30

party 7, 19, 20–21

Pilgrims 11, 12, 16, 17, 18, 19, 20, 22, 26, 30

Plymouth Bay, Massachusetts 9, 10, 15, 30

Puritans 12–13, 14

Tisquantum (Squanto) 17, 18

turkey 5, 6, 18, 21

United States 8, 22, 26

Wampanoag 9, 17, 19, 20